Real Life Stories

HOMESTEADING

Jill Foran

— Weigl Publishers Inc. —

About *Homesteading*

This book is based on the real life accounts of the people who settled the American West. History is brought to life through quotes from personal journals, letters to family back home, and historical records of those who traveled West to build a better life.

Published by Weigl Publishers Inc.
123 South Broad Street, Box 227
Mankato, MN 56002
USA

Web site: www.weigl.com

Library of Congress Cataloging-in-Publication Data

Foran, Jill.
  Homesteading / Jill Foran.
     p. cm. -- (Real life stories series)
Summary: Brief text chronicles the activities of the homesteaders who settled the vast American prairies during the late nineteenth and early twentieth centuries. Features first-hand accounts. Includes bibliographical references and index.
  ISBN 1-59036-079-6 (Library Bound : alk. paper)
 1. Frontier and pioneer life--West (U.S.)--Juvenile literature. 2. Pioneers--West (U.S.)--History--19th century--Juvenile literature. 3. West (U.S.)--History--19th century--Juvenile literature. 4. West (U.S.)--Social life and customs--19th century--Juvenile literature. [1. Frontier and pioneer life--West (U.S.) 2. West (U.S.)--History--19th century. 3. West (U.S.)--Social life and customs.] I. Title. II. Series.
  F596 .F623 2003
  978'.02--dc21

                              2002012724

Printed in the United States of America
1 2 3 4 5 6 7 8 9 0   06 05 04 03 02

Photograph Credits
Cover: CORBIS/MAGMA; **Canadian Pacific Railway Archives:** page 4 (NS.8454); **Comstock, Inc.:** page 21; **Corbis Corporation:** page 14; **Fred Hultstrand History in Pictures Collections, Institute for Regional Studies & University Archives, North Dakota State University:** pages 1 (2028.061), 6 (2028.108), 8 (2028.261), 10 (2028.459), 12/13 (2028.115); **Glenbow Archives:** pages 3 (NA-3718-2), 16 (NA-3974-2), 21 (NA-3961-4), 22 (NA-2299-10); **Library of Congress:** page 18 (LC-USZ62-104167).

Text Credits
Excerpt on page 17: Ingalls Wilder, Laura. *On the Banks of Plum Creek*. New York: HarperCollins Juvenile Books, 1953.

Project Coordinator	**Copy Editor**	**Layout**
Michael Lowry	Heather Kissock	Terry Paulhus
Substantive Editor	**Design**	**Photo Research**
Christa Bedry	Virginia Boulay & Bryan Pezzi	Dylan Kirk & Daorcey Le Bray

Contents

A New Life

The United States government announced that free land was available in the **West** in 1862. This **declaration** was called the Homestead Act. The act attracted people from all over the world. People traveled to the West to begin new lives. These people were called homesteaders. They worked very hard. They built their homes and farmed their land.

WE'RE SAILING WEST. WE'RE SAILING WEST. TO PRAIRIE LANDS SUNKISSED AND BLEST— THE CROFTER'S TRAIL TO HAPPINESS.

Some homesteaders traveled from Europe to begin a new life in the West.

Rules of the Homestead Act

The Homestead Act drew millions of people to the West. Homesteaders were given free land as long as they followed the rules set by the government.

- Homesteaders had to be at least 21 years old.

- Each homesteader could claim 160 acres of land.

- The homesteader had to build a house on the land.

- Each homesteader had to dig a water well on the land.

- The homesteader had to farm at least 10 acres of the land.

- The homesteader could own the land after 5 years of living on it.

Standing Room Only

Many early homesteaders lived in homes made of **sod**. They lived in sod houses because there was little wood available. Sod houses leaked when it rained. Rats, snakes, and insects lived in the sod walls. The houses were very small. Families did not have much room in which to move.

The tiny houses were often very crowded. Family members had to stand while they ate their meals.

Real Life Stories

*"The whole family lived, ate, and slept in the same room. There was far too little space for each member of the family to have a separate bed. Adults and children slept wherever they could, most often on blankets or straw mattresses laid on the floor. The **dugout** was little more than a hole in the ground, covered over with wood and earth to keep out the weather. Families lived for years in these homes before they could build better ones."*

Unknown Homesteader

Neighbors in Need

Early **settlers** felt quite alone. Homesteads were often miles apart. Still, neighbors made an effort to see each other. Neighbors shared farm work. They helped each other build homes and gather the crops. They ran errands for each other. Neighbors held large parties for holidays and weddings.

Homesteaders often helped each other build homes and barns. How can sharing work with friends help complete the task?

Real Life Stories

*"The homesteaders were very sociable … helping each other in sickness and when one neighbor would drive to town … 25 miles away … they would bring groceries, medicine, mail, or whatever was needed for all. I remember one time my husband went into town in a bobsled, coming home his **endgate** lost out and scattered groceries for a long way, so he had to go back and gather them up … it usually took 2 days to make a trip."*

Mary Ann Burbank Williams

Life on the Prairies

Homesteaders living on the **prairies** faced many challenges. The land often lacked water and trees. Crops were ruined when there was not enough rain in spring and summer. Homesteaders could not always find wood for shelter and fuel. Many settlers burned buffalo and cow **chips** for fuel instead of wood. Collecting and burning the chips were not pleasant tasks. Settlers used chips because they kept homes warm throughout winter.

Many homesteaders used baskets to carry their goods.

Real Life Stories

"Each [cow chip] picker would tie a rope to the handle of an old washtub and pull it around over the grass and pick up all the chips they could find. They would fill the tubs, then empty them into the wagon until it was full. Then it was unloaded in a pile. This operation was repeated [until] a pile of chips [was] built up to 10 [to] 12 feet long and as high as they could be piled … Some job, but if we could find plenty of chips we were warm and comfortable."

Orval Lookhart

The Homestead

Early homesteads in the West were very simple. Families that settled on the prairies had very little money. They had to live plainly. Furniture and decorations were homemade. Rooms were lit with candles or oil lamps. Washrooms were located outside of the house.

The kitchen was the most important room in the house. It contained a large fireplace.

The inside walls were covered with a mixture of ash and clay. This kept insects out.

The thick walls were made of **turf**. Turf walls helped keep the house warm in winter and cool in summer.

Most farmhouses were made of sod. Only farmers with a great deal of money could afford to build log cabins.

Roofs were layered with hay, twigs, and small branches. These materials were covered with turf.

The floors were made of dirt. Beds and sleeping bunks were placed in the corners of the floor or built into the walls.

Disaster Strikes!

Homesteaders worked hard to develop their farms. They were able to grow many grains, fruits, and vegetables when the weather was good. Some homesteaders raised animals. Blizzards, tornadoes, and **droughts** often led to hard times. Huge groups of insects ruined crops. Some groups of grasshoppers were so large that they darkened the sky.

Bad weather ruined crops and damaged homesteads. How would this tornado affect a farm or a house?

Real Life Stories

"In … October 1867, the [grass]hoppers came the first time. They were so thick that you could scrape them up … by the shovel-full. [We] couldn't keep them out of our faces as we walked along. They stayed long [enough] to lay the ground full of eggs, and we had a big [group] of grasshoppers the next year and they took the early crop as fast as they could. The … [grass]hoppers stayed until harvest, [and they did] all they could to harvest the crop … After they flew away, we thought goodbye, but no, here they came again and filled the ground with eggs for three years."

Jane Metcalf Jolliffe

Fun on the Farm

Homesteading was difficult. The adults worked very hard. They built their homes and looked after their farms. The children had many chores. They helped take care of the crops, feed the animals, and cleaned the house. The children also found time to have fun. Settler children played hide-and-seek and leapfrog when the work was done. They also played blindman's bluff and pussy-in-the-corner. The children would toboggan and ice-skate in the winter.

Swimming in rivers or ponds helped children stay cool and have fun on hot, summer days.

Real Life Stories

"Laura stood in one corner, Mary in another, and Carrie in a third. There were only three corners, because the stove was in one. Ma stood in the middle of the floor and cried, 'Poor pussy wants a corner!'

Then all at once they ran out of their corners and each tried to get into another corner … Ma dodged into Mary's corner, and that left Mary out to be poor pussy. Then Laura fell … and that left Laura out. Carrie ran laughing into the wrong corners at first, but she soon learned. They ran until they were gasping from running and shouting and laughing."

Laura Ingalls Wilder

The First Free Homestead

Daniel Freeman was the first person to claim free land after the Homestead Act of 1862. Daniel went to Nebraska to search for the land he wanted. He received 160 acres of free land days later. Nebraska was the site of the first free homestead in the United States.

More than 2 million people filed for free land after Daniel Freeman.

Number of Homesteaders in 1870 and 1900

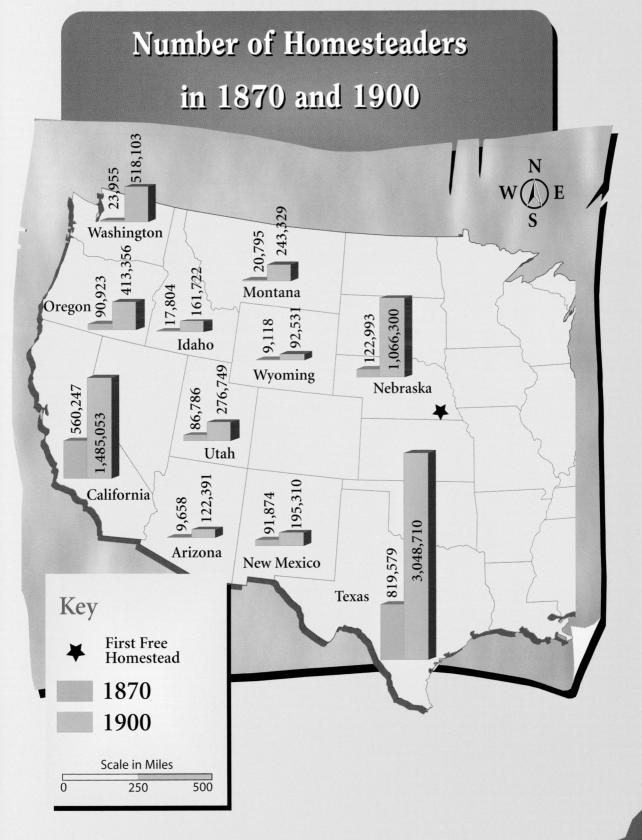

Washington — 23,955 / 518,103

Oregon — 90,923 / 413,356

Idaho — 17,804 / 161,722

Montana — 20,795 / 243,329

Wyoming — 9,118 / 92,531

Nebraska — 122,993 / 1,066,300

California — 560,247 / 1,485,053

Utah — 86,786 / 276,749

Arizona — 9,658 / 122,391

New Mexico — 91,874 / 195,310

Texas — 819,579 / 3,048,710

Key

★ First Free Homestead

1870

1900

Scale in Miles

0   250   500

Learning More about Homesteading

To learn more about homesteading, you can borrow books from the library or surf the Internet.

Books

Ingalls Wilder, Laura. *Laura's Early Years Collection.* New York: HarperCollins Juvenile Books, 1999.

Taylor, Sherri Peel. *Pioneers of the American West.* San Diego: Lucent Books, 2001.

Web Sites

Frontier House
www.pbs.org/wnet/frontierhouse/
The Frontier House Web site takes visitors on a virtual journey of early settler life.

Encarta
www.encarta.com
Enter the search word "homesteading" into an online encyclopedia, such as Encarta.

Compare and Contrast

Life in the 1880s was very different from life today. Use the information in this book, along with Internet or library research. Compare your life at home with the lives of early homesteading families. How is your life different from theirs? How is it the same? Create a chart or a poster that compares your life to homesteading life.

What Have You Learned?

Based on what you have just read, try to answer the following questions.

1 Which material was used to build many early homes on the prairies?

a) wood   b) bricks
c) sod   d) stones

2 Which state is home to the country's first free homestead?

a) Colorado
b) Nebraska
c) Kansas
d) Wyoming

3
Which insects caused great damage to crops?

a) grasshoppers　　b) butterflies

c) mosquitoes　　d) bees

4
True or False?
The children of homesteaders did not have time for fun and games. They were too busy helping with housework and farm work.

5
True or False? Many homesteaders burned cow chips for heat and fuel.

6
True or False? Neighboring homesteaders lived so far from each other that they rarely visited each other.

Words to Know

chips: dried animal dung

declaration: official announcement

droughts: long periods without rain

dugout: house that is dug out of the ground

endgate: gate at the back of a wagon that allows loading and unloading

prairies: flat, treeless lands

settlers: people who set up their homes in a new region

sod: piece of grassy ground

turf: layers of earth formed from grass and plant roots

West: region of the United States west of the Mississippi River

Index